The Great Character Development Workbook

Accountability	Concentration	Ethics	Industriousness	Perseverance	Satisfaction
Accuracy	Confidence	Excellence	Influence	Personality	Security
Achievement	Conscience	Fairness	Ingenuity	Persuasiveness	Self Esteem
Acknowledgement	Consistency	Faith	Initiative	Planning	Sensitivity
Adaptability	Conservation	Fidelity	Innovation	Poise	Sharing
Affection	Contentment	Fitness	Insight	Politeness	Sincerity
Altruism	Conviction	Flexibility	Inspiration	Potential	Skepticism
Ambition	Cooperation	Focus	Integrity	Practice	Spirituality
Appearance	Courage	Foresight	Intelligence	Praise	Sportsmanship
Appreciation	Creativity	Forgiveness	Intuition	Preparedness	Stability
Appropriate	Curiosity	Fortitude	Investment	Preservation	Strength
Articulate	Decency	Friendship	Justice	Prevention	Sympathy
Assertiveness	Dedication	Fulfillment	Kindness	Pride	Tact
Attitude	Dependability	Generosity	Leadership	Priorities	Talent
Awareness	Determination	Gentleness	Love	Privacy	Teamwork
Balance	Devotion	Goals	Loyalty	Proactive	Tenacity
Benevolence	Dignity	Grace	Maturity	Professionalism	Timing
Boundaries	Diligence	Graciousness	Moderation	Proficiency	Tolerance
Challenge	Diplomacy	Gratitude	Modesty	Punctuality	Trust
Charity	Discipline	Happiness	Morality	Readiness	Trustworthiness
Citizenship	Discretion	Heroism	Motivation	Reasonableness	Truth
Civility	Diversity	Honesty	Neatness	Recognition	Variety
Cleanliness	Efficiency	Honor	Objectivity	Reconciliation	Veracity
Commitment	Effort	Hospitality	Openness	Reliability	Vision
Common Sense	Empathy	Humility	Optimism	Reputation	Visualization
Communication	Empowerment	Humor	Organization	Resilience	Vitality
Compassion	Encouragement	Imagination	Ownership	Resourcefulness	Willingness
Compatibility	Endurance	Improvement	Passion	Respect	Willpower
Competence	Energy	Improvisation	Patience	Responsibility	Wisdom
Composure	Enthusiasm	Independence	Patriotism	Restraint	Youthfulness
Compromise	Equality	Individuality	Performance	Sacrifice	Zeal

This educational workbook is designed to encourage young people to build personal character development. Each one of the listed 186 values, virtues, traits, ethics, morals and assets is described with a simple definition and used in a sentence to illustrate their proper context. These definitions are very basic; look in a dictionary for more details or to explore other meanings that some of these words may have. You do not have to complete the pages in any specific order. To help track your progress you can circle or highlight the words on the master word list as you finish them.

This workbook requires active participation from two people; the child and an adult, peer, or role model who can share and demonstrate examples of the concepts, principles, and actions that these character-building words represent.

Try to incorporate into your regular vocabulary and behavior these positive character traits. Knowing about them is important, but it is essential that good character development is actively encouraged and used frequently so the actions become an integral facet of your life. Thank you for your dedication to complete this book. I am confident that your great character development will have positive effects in all areas of your life.

www.thegreatcharacterdevelopmentworkbook.com
Copyright © 2003 The Great Character Development Workbook
Written and Published by Nick Hoke in Kingston, Washington. Printed in the United States: ISBN 0-9728417-0-9
All rights reserved. No part of this publication may be reproduced, stored in a retrieval system or transmitted in any form or by any means electronic, mechanical, photocopying, recording or otherwise, without the prior written permission of the publisher.

Accountability

Accountability is being trusted with responsibility. *Simon knew he would be held accountable if anything went wrong at the house while his parents were away.*

Describe an example when someone you know was held accountable for something:

_____
_____
_____

Write about a time you were held accountable:

_____
_____
_____

Accuracy

Accuracy is being precise, exact, and free from mistake or error. *Carter was good at mathematics because he was very accurate with his calculations.*

Describe a time when someone did something with accuracy:

_____
_____
_____

Write about a time when you used accuracy:

_____
_____
_____

Achievement

Achievement is the act of gaining something by successfully accomplishing a goal. *Heidi achieved her goal of earning a position on the team by going to all the workouts.*

When did someone you know achieve something:

_____
_____
_____

Write about something you achieved:

_____
_____
_____

Acknowledgement

Acknowledgement is admitting something or recognizing someone. *Leah felt pretty good after her supervisor acknowledged her efforts with a compliment.*

Describe a situation where someone acknowledged something or someone:
_____
_____
_____

When did you show acknowledgement:
_____
_____
_____

Adaptability

Adaptability is the ability to change or be changed to fit a situation. *Susan showed adaptability when she was able to adjust to the new work schedule without complaining.*

Describe a time someone showed adaptability:
_____
_____
_____

When was a time you adapted to something:
_____
_____
_____

Affection

Affection is the expression of warm, pleasant feelings or emotions for someone or something. *Elizabeth showed her affection for her neighbors by bringing them home baked cookies.*

When did someone you know show affection:
_____
_____
_____

When did you show affection:
_____
_____
_____

Altruism

Altruism is unselfish, generous concern for the welfare of others. *Hudson was well known as being very altruistic; he volunteered at a synagogue and homeless shelter for years.*

Describe an instance when someone you know acted with altruism:

_____
_____
_____

What did you do that was altruistic:

_____
_____
_____

Ambition

Ambition is an eager and strong desire to achieve something. *Michael's ambition to raise a lot of money for the victim's program was inspiring to his friends.*

Write about a time someone you know showed ambition:

_____
_____
_____

When did you have ambition:

_____
_____
_____

Appearance

Appearance is how you present yourself to others, or how they view you. *Meredith knew that her customers would judge her right away by her appearance.*

Write about a time someone's appearance caused people to think something about them:

_____
_____
_____

Write about a time your appearance influenced people to think something about you:

_____
_____
_____

Appreciation

Appreciation is having or showing awareness and recognition. *Logan appreciated the way his teacher made time for his special project.*

Write about a time someone you know showed appreciation:

_____
_____
_____

Write about a time you showed appreciation:

_____
_____
_____

Appropriate

Appropriate is something suitable and correct for a particular person, place or condition. *Jill knew that it was not appropriate to let her little brothers play with their father's tools.*

Write about a time someone did something appropriate:

_____
_____
_____

When did you do something that was appropriate:

_____
_____
_____

Articulate

Being articulate is speaking distinctly, clearly, and expressively. *Because he was an articulate speaker, Darrin was able to convince his neighbors to organize a block watch program.*

Write about a time someone was articulate:

_____
_____
_____

When were you articulate:

_____
_____
_____

Assertiveness

Assertiveness is confidently demonstrating positive self-assurance. *Greta refused the cigarette in an assertive manner by saying "no" in a very firm but polite way.*

Describe a time when somebody showed assertiveness:
_____
_____
_____

When were you assertive:
_____
_____
_____

Attitude

Attitude is the manner in which you present your beliefs and feelings to others. *Kyesha's positive attitude about her job made everybody happy to have her working with them.*

Describe an attitude somebody showed:
_____
_____
_____

When did your attitude affect somebody else:
_____
_____
_____

Awareness

Awareness is having knowledge of what is going on around you. Natasha was aware that her parents were having communication problems with each other.

Write about a time when someone showed awareness:
_____
_____
_____

Write about a time when you had awareness:
_____
_____
_____

Balance

Balance is having certain parts of your life in an equal and satisfying state of harmony and proportion. *Although Diosdado worked hard, he knew that he needed a good balance in his life between work and recreation.*

Describe someone who showed balance in his or her life:
_____
_____
_____

Describe an example of balance in your life:
_____
_____
_____

Benevolence

Benevolence is performing kind, charitable acts. *Mrs. Davis was recognized as a benevolent contributor to the animal shelter after she donated a large amount of money to their program.*

Write about a time someone acted benevolently:
_____
_____
_____

Write about a time you showed benevolence:
_____
_____
_____

Boundaries

Boundaries are established limits. *Lisa told her clients that there were boundaries that needed to be respected during certain conversation topics.*

Describe a time when somebody had boundaries:
_____
_____
_____

Write about a time you had boundaries:
_____
_____
_____

Challenge

Challenge is a demanding test of one's abilities. *Nyela was not content with her current job; she wanted one that was more difficult and would challenge her mind more.*

When did you see someone challenged:
_____
_____
_____

Describe a challenge you dealt with:
_____
_____
_____

Charity

Charity is showing generosity by giving things to people who need help. *Cameron demonstrated charity when she volunteered with her church group to help clean the garden at the nursing home.*

When did you see someone show charity:
_____
_____
_____

When did you do something charitable:
_____
_____
_____

Citizenship

Citizenship is being a responsible and contributing member of society. *Because Savannah obeyed all the laws, paid her taxes, and volunteered in her community, she was respected as a good citizen.*

Write about a person who demonstrated good citizenship:
_____
_____
_____

What have you done to be a good citizen:
_____
_____
_____

Civility

Civility is courteous, polite behavior. *Mark did not like the morning delivery man's attitude but he always smiled and acted with civility towards him.*

Write about someone who acted with civility:
___
___
___

When did you show civility:
___
___
___

Cleanliness

Cleanliness is being neat and clean. *Renee's brother told her that her life would be easier if she maintained a higher level of cleanliness and organization.*

Give an example about a person who practiced cleanliness:
___
___
___

Describe a time you showed cleanliness:
___
___
___

Commitment

Commitment is an agreement or pledge to do something in the future. *Robin made a commitment to help her little brother with his homework when he needed it.*

Write about a time somebody fulfilled a commitment:
___
___
___

Write about a time you showed commitment:
___
___
___

Common Sense

Common sense is sound, practical judgment. *Bob used common sense when the strange dog approached him; he did not pet it.*

Write about a time someone used common sense:
___
___
___

When did you use common sense:
___
___
___

Communication

Communication is effective sharing of messages and information. *The counselor helped Martha and her husband realize that a frequent problem in their relationship was a lack of clear communication.*

Write about someone who demonstrated good communication:
___
___
___

Describe an incident when communication was important:
___
___
___

Compassion

Compassion is being aware of suffering and having a strong desire to fix the problem. *Madeline showed a great amount of compassion for the sick children by the way she spent so much time caring for them.*

Describe an example when someone showed compassion:
___
___
___

Write about a time you were compassionate:
___
___
___

Compatibility

Compatibility is being able to get along with others in a pleasant and harmonious manner. *Because Rachel and her friends shared the same interests and hobbies, they all agreed that they were compatible with each other.*

Write about someone who showed compatibility:

_____
_____
_____

Write about a time you were compatible with someone:

_____
_____
_____

Competence

Competence is having the necessary abilities, skills, or knowledge to perform a task. *Farisa was very competent at saving and investing her extra money.*

Describe a person who was competent at something:

_____
_____
_____

Write about a time you showed competence:

_____
_____
_____

Composure

Composure is the state of being and acting calm. *Andrew showed steady composure during the crisis, which helped the other people to stay calm and not panic.*

Write about a time when someone showed composure:

_____
_____
_____

When did you have composure:

_____
_____
_____

Compromise

Compromise is a mutual promise or agreement to resolve a difference. *Amelia's compromise with her parents meant that she could stay out later on Saturday night, as long as she called home a couple of times.*

Write about someone who made a compromise:

_____
_____
_____

How did you make a compromise:

_____
_____
_____

Concentration

Concentration is the act or process of being able to focus attention on one thing. *Carrie used three decks of playing cards to make a card house; balancing and stacking them all required a fair amount of concentration.*

Write about someone who showed concentration:

_____
_____
_____

When did you use concentration:

_____
_____
_____

Confidence

Confidence is faith, trust, and assurance in a person or thing. *Because Melissa always completed her homework, she was confident she would earn a high grade.*

Write about a person who showed confidence:

_____
_____
_____

Write about a time you had confidence:

_____
_____
_____

Conscience

Conscience is knowing and feeling the difference between what is right and wrong. *Jamie knew she would have a guilty conscience if she chose to copy Erin's homework.*

Write about a time a person followed their conscience:
_____
_____
_____

When did you listen to your conscience:
_____
_____
_____

Consistency

Consistency is being reliable all the time. *Jerome knew that consistent parenting rules were necessary for the proper growth and development of his children.*

Describe someone who did something with consistency:
_____
_____
_____

What did you do with consistency:
_____
_____
_____

Conservation

Conservation is the act of preserving something from loss, damage or neglect. *Kim never let the water run while she brushed her teeth; she conserved the water.*

Describe somebody you know who practiced conservation:
_____
_____
_____

When did you show conservation:
_____
_____
_____

Contentment

Contentment is the state being satisfied. *When all the housework was done and the bills were paid at the end of the week, Pat felt a deep contentment about his life.*

Write about a person who had contentment:

_____
_____
_____

When were you content:

_____
_____
_____

Conviction

Conviction is having a strong belief or attitude toward something. *Xavier had a strong conviction that he should always be a positive influence to his younger brothers because they always looked up to him.*

Write about a person who had conviction about something:

_____
_____
_____

What did you do with conviction about:

_____
_____
_____

Cooperation

Cooperation is working with others to achieve a common goal. *Carlos knew he would have to cooperate with his uncle when they both volunteered to fix the old broken table.*

Describe a time when someone you know showed cooperation:

_____
_____
_____

When did you cooperate with another person:

_____
_____
_____

Courage

Courage is feeling or acting brave when you feel afraid in a difficult situation. *Stella showed courage when she convinced her best friend to get help for her drug problem.*

Describe somebody who did something with courage:

_____
_____
_____

What did you do that required courage:

_____
_____
_____

Creativity

Creativity is expressing yourself in an original and unique way. *When Brett colored his artwork differently than his classmates, the teacher commented on his creativity.*

Write about someone you know who showed creativity:

_____
_____
_____

What did you do with creativity:

_____
_____
_____

Curiosity

Curiosity is having a strong, inquisitive desire to learn and gain knowledge. *Chris's curiosity about the endangered birds eventually influenced him to volunteer at the wildlife sanctuary.*

Describe someone you know who acted on curiosity:

_____
_____
_____

When did you have curiosity:

_____
_____
_____

Decency

Decency is being nice and polite. *Linda showed decency in the awkward situation when she suddenly met the man who had hit her brother.*

Describe an instance when someone demonstrated decency:
___
___
___

When did you do something with decency:
___
___
___

Dedication

Dedication is selfless devotion to something or someone. *Emily was very dedicated to her academic success and the results showed it.*

Write about a person who showed dedication:
___
___
___

When did you do something with dedication:
___
___
___

Dependability

Dependability is regularly doing something that is expected. *Because Malcolm always arrived at his job early every day, his coworkers knew they could depend upon him to start the machines on time.*

Describe a person who showed dependability:
___
___
___

When did you demonstrate dependability:
___
___
___

Determination

Determination is having a firm intention to achieve a goal. *Yuriko was determined to find out why some of the kids were acting out in an aggressive manner.*

Write about a person who showed determination:

_____
_____
_____

What did you do with determination:

_____
_____
_____

Devotion

Devotion is having a selfless and dedicated affection toward a person or a cause. *Bryan is devoted to his wife's happiness and personal growth.*

Write about a person who showed devotion:

_____
_____
_____

When did you have devotion:

_____
_____
_____

Dignity

Dignity is the correct and mature behavior or appearance for a situation. *With a gracious smile, Valerie showed dignity when she unexpectedly lost the spelling bee contest.*

Write about someone who showed dignity:

_____
_____
_____

What did you do with dignity:

_____
_____
_____

Diligence

Diligence is working toward a goal with steady and persistent effort. *Jeff showed diligence by always going to his neighbors' houses on garbage day to help them with their heavy garbage cans.*

Describe a person who did something with diligence:

_____
_____
_____

What did you do that showed diligence:

_____
_____
_____

Diplomacy

Diplomacy is the art or practice of dealing with people with skill and tact. *Mona showed diplomacy when she approached the other parents and talked to them about the bad behavior of their children.*

Write about a person who did something with diplomacy:

_____
_____
_____

Describe a time you showed diplomacy:

_____
_____
_____

Discipline

Discipline is using consistent and self controlled effort to accomplish a goal. *William had the discipline to get up on time every morning all by himself.*

Write about a person who showed discipline in doing something:

_____
_____
_____

When did you do something with discipline:

_____
_____
_____

Discretion

Discretion is the ability to be discreet and cautious when addressing an issue. *Joanie showed discretion by waiting until she was alone with her daughter to bring up the sensitive subject.*

Write about a time someone acted with discretion:

_____
_____
_____

When did you act with discretion:

_____
_____
_____

Diversity

Diversity is being made up of many different and distinct qualities or characteristics. *Eric enjoyed the great diversity of his team members and he appreciated their individual differences.*

Describe somebody you know who dealt with diversity:

_____
_____
_____

Write about a time you valued diversity:

_____
_____
_____

Efficiency

Efficiency is doing something effectively by wasting or losing as little as possible. *Phoebe's efficiency at starting and finishing her chores and homework on time had a positive influence on her little brother.*

Write about someone who did something with efficiency:

_____
_____
_____

Write about a time you were efficient:

_____
_____
_____

Effort

Effort is the use of physical or mental energy to accomplish something. *Shawna's grandparents made an effort to explain to her how her actions affected the way other people judged her personality and character.*

Write about someone who did something with effort:

___
___
___

Describe something you did with effort:

___
___
___

Empathy

Empathy is identification with and understanding of another's situation, feelings, and motives. *Daniel showed empathy for the frustration his friend felt about being pushed around at school by a bully.*

Describe someone you know who showed empathy:

___
___
___

When did you show empathy:

___
___
___

Empowerment

Empowerment is to gain power or authority. *Dominque taught his cousin several new coping skills that empowered him to deal with adversity in appropriate ways.*

Describe a time when someone had empowerment:

___
___
___

When did you receive or grant empowerment:

___
___
___

Encouragement

Encouragement is expressing approval and support to give someone hope. *When Scott's wife decided to open her own store, he gave her lots of help and encouragement.*

When did somebody give you encouragement:

_____
_____
_____

When did you show encouragement:

_____
_____
_____

Endurance

Endurance is the quality or action of not giving up while facing stress, hardship, or adversity. *Tony needed endurance to finish the race.*

Write about a time someone showed endurance:

_____
_____
_____

When did you show endurance:

_____
_____
_____

Energy

Energy is the capacity for being active and doing things. *One of the reasons why Conchita was a good elementary school teacher was because she had lots of energy to keep her students interested in the lessons.*

When did you see somebody with energy:

_____
_____
_____

Write about a something you did with energy:

_____
_____
_____

Enthusiasm

Enthusiasm is having great excitement and energy for something. *Kip was enthusiastic about soliciting people to help donate money for the new animal shelter.*

Write about someone who had enthusiasm:

_____
_____
_____

What were you enthusiastic about:

_____
_____
_____

Equality

Equality is the state of being alike or the same; neither inferior nor superior. *Lance did not care why or how people were different from him; he treated them all with equality.*

Write about someone who practices equality:

_____
_____
_____

How did you demonstrate equality:

_____
_____
_____

Ethics

Ethics are the rules, standards, and morals that govern a person's conduct. *Because Gordon never made personal phone calls from work, his employer appreciated his ethical behavior.*

Write about a person who showed ethics:

_____
_____
_____

Describe something you did that was ethical:

_____
_____
_____

Excellence

Excellence is the state, quality, or condition of doing something with greatness. *Thomas worked for excellence by always trying to do his best.*

Write about a person who did something with excellence:

_____

_____

_____

When did you show excellence:

_____

_____

_____

Fairness

Fairness is being consistent and applying the same rules and standards for everybody. *Kolechko always showed fairness when he disciplined the students; none of them received preferential or harsh treatment.*

When did you see someone show fairness:

_____

_____

_____

When did you treat someone with fairness:

_____

_____

_____

Faith

Faith is a confident belief in the truth, value, or trustworthiness of a person, an idea, or a thing. *Nita had faith that the disabled veterans would really enjoy the student's patriotic essays.*

Write about someone who had faith in something:

_____

_____

_____

Write about something you had faith in:

_____

_____

_____

Fidelity

Fidelity is unfailing faithfulness and strict adherence to vows or promises. *Ginny showed fidelity in her relationship with her new boyfriend; she did not hang around with any other boys.*

Write about someone who showed fidelity:

_____
_____
_____

What did you do with fidelity:

_____
_____
_____

Fitness

Fitness is the state of being in a good physical condition. *Evelyn attributed her high level of physical fitness to daily exercise and a moderate consumption of unhealthy snacks.*

Write about someone who showed fitness:

_____
_____
_____

What did you do to improve your fitness:

_____
_____
_____

Flexibility

Flexibility is being responsive and adaptable to a changing situation. *Lofton was bothered by the delays but because he was flexible he told the manager that he would still be able to work efficiently with the new schedule.*

Write about someone who was flexible:

_____
_____
_____

When did you show flexibility:

_____
_____
_____

Focus

Focus is concentrating attention or energy toward a goal. *Ian knew he had to focus on thinking about the consequences of what the boys were asking him to do.*

When did you see somebody show focus:
_____
_____
_____

Write about a time you had focus:
_____
_____
_____

Foresight

Foresight is being able to perceive and recognize the significance of an event or an action before it happens. *Oscar had the foresight to realize that eating a lot of junk food at the party would probably make him sick.*

Write about a time someone showed foresight:
_____
_____
_____

When did you have foresight:
_____
_____
_____

Forgiveness

Forgiveness is the ending of feeling resentment against someone. *After Carol talked to her rabbi, she decided to accept her cousin's apology and forgive him.*

Describe a time when someone you know demonstrated forgiveness:
_____
_____
_____

When did you show forgiveness:
_____
_____
_____

Fortitude

Fortitude is having mental strength to endure pain or adversity with courage. *Kalei's strong will and fortitude was noticed by everybody who visited her in the hospital.*

Write about someone who showed fortitude:
_____
_____
_____

What did you do with fortitude:
_____
_____
_____

Friendship

Friendship is the relationship between friends. *Isaiah valued Chuck's friendship when he realized that there could be a big difference between friends who were good for each other and friends who were just fun.*

When did you see an example of friendship:
_____
_____
_____

Write about a friendship that you have:
_____
_____
_____

Fulfillment

Fulfillment is the action of finishing something or carrying out a promise. *Tegan fulfilled her promise to let her parents know that she had arrived at her friend's house safely and on time.*

Describe someone who demonstrated fulfillment:
_____
_____
_____

Describe a goal or promise that you fulfilled:
_____
_____
_____

Generosity

Generosity is having a willingness to give and share with others. *Gunnar's mother had a great amount of generosity, especially with her hugs.*

Describe somebody who demonstrated generosity:
_____
_____
_____

What did you do that was generous:
_____
_____
_____

Gentleness

Gentleness is being kind, considerate, gentle and tender. *Katie's warm gentleness as a counselor was always helpful and appreciated.*

Write about someone who showed gentleness:
_____
_____
_____

When did you demonstrate gentleness:
_____
_____
_____

Goals

Goals are the purpose toward which an endeavor or objective is directed. *One of Malachi's goals was to work hard on his school project every afternoon, before he went out to play.*

Write about somebody's goals:
_____
_____
_____

What are some of your goals:
_____
_____
_____

Grace

Grace is a social behavior that reflects charm, beauty, and elegance. *Vedrana walked and talked with grace, and everybody agreed that she was a beautiful person.*

Write about someone who demonstrated grace:
_____
_____
_____

What did you do with grace:
_____
_____
_____

Graciousness

Graciousness is behavior that is kind, warm, and courteous. *Jennifer received the boy's presents with graciousness and many words of thanks.*

Describe an example when somebody showed graciousness:
_____
_____
_____

When did you do something gracious:
_____
_____
_____

Gratitude

Gratitude is showing the state of being appreciative, thankful and grateful. *Sasha showed her gratitude to the volunteers by bringing them cups of water and orange slices.*

Write about someone who showed gratitude:
_____
_____
_____

How did you show gratitude:
_____
_____
_____

Happiness

Happiness is a state of personal well being and contentment. *Walt had been happy in his life and he had been sad, and knew that he liked happiness much more than sadness.*

Describe someone who showed happiness:
_____
_____
_____

When did you have happiness:
_____
_____
_____

Heroism

Heroism is self sacrificing, courageous conduct. *When Becky protected her little sister from the mean dogs, everybody said it was a heroic act.*

Write about a person who showed heroism:
_____
_____
_____

When did you do something heroic:
_____
_____
_____

Honesty

Honesty is truthful conduct and sincere adherence to facts. *Rob knew that honesty with his parents was always the best policy, even when being honest with them was hard to do.*

Write about a person who showed honesty:
_____
_____
_____

When did you do something honest:
_____
_____
_____

Honor

Honor is a strong sense of ethical conduct. *Lynette's friends said she had strong sense of honor because she never promised to do anything that she could not or would not do.*

Write about someone who did something with honor:

_____

_____

_____

When did you act with honor:

_____

_____

_____

Hospitality

Hospitality is being generous and sharing toward guests. *Dayle was a very good host to her visiting friends; they were thankful for her warm hospitality.*

Describe an example when someone you know showed hospitality:

_____

_____

_____

When did you show hospitality:

_____

_____

_____

Humility

Humility is being humble and not boasting or bragging. *When Chelsea got in trouble for breaking the rules, she quietly accepted her punishment with humility and she did not protest loudly or make a big scene in the office.*

When did you see someone act with humility:

_____

_____

_____

When did you show humility:

_____

_____

_____

Humor

Humor is recognizing and appreciating something funny. *Margaret had a great sense of humor; she always appreciated a good joke if it didn't hurt or offend anybody.*

Write about a person who had good humor:
_____
_____
_____

What did you do to show good humor in a situation:
_____
_____
_____

Imagination

Imagination is the creative ability to think of new ideas, images, or concepts. *One of the reasons why George was such a good businessman was because he used his imagination to think of new ways to sell his products.*

Write about someone who had imagination:
_____
_____
_____

When did you use imagination:
_____
_____
_____

Improvement

Improvement is to make or enhance something to make it better. *John never hesitated to ask his parents for advice; he knew that he needed improvement with his advocacy skills.*

Describe a time someone showed improvement:
_____
_____
_____

When did you show improvement:
_____
_____
_____

Improvisation

Improvisation is creating something with limited resources. *When Diego used different parts to finish his art project, his teacher gave him extra points for improvisation.*

Write about someone who improvised something:

_____
_____
_____

When did you improvise something:

_____
_____
_____

Independence

Independence is having freedom from relying on or being controlled by other people. *Andrea was independent enough to finish her chores without asking for help.*

Write about a person who did something with independence:

_____
_____
_____

When did you show independence:

_____
_____
_____

Individuality

Individuality is the unique set of qualities that make each person different and distinct from each other. *Morgan showed her individuality when she was the only one who wrote a paper protesting the new and unpopular rules.*

Write about a person who showed individuality:

_____
_____
_____

What did you do to assert your individuality:

_____
_____
_____

Industriousness

Industriousness is working hard and diligently in an intelligent manner. *Kirk showed a lot of creative energy at the lab, and despite the limited resources, his industriousness allowed the experiments to proceed along.*

Describe an example when someone showed industriousness:
___
___
___

Write about a time when you showed industriousness:
___
___
___

Influence

Influence is the ability to cause a change without using physical strength. *Paul used his strong influence as a big brother to remind his sister that she should never touch their grandparent's handguns.*

Describe somebody's influence on you:
___
___
___

When did you have an influence on someone else:
___
___
___

Ingenuity

Ingenuity is being skilful or clever in doing something. *Alicia showed ingenuity by the many different reasons she gave her friends when she answered why she would not try the cigarette.*

When did someone show ingenuity:
___
___
___

When did you do something with ingenuity:
___
___
___

Initiative

Initiative is the action of starting something without prompting. *Gary took the initiative to put sunscreen on himself before his brother had to remind him.*

Write about a person who showed initiative:
_____
_____
_____

How did you show initiative:
_____
_____
_____

Innovation

Innovation is doing something in a new way. *Angela's skillful methods of preparing the vegetables were an innovative way to encourage the children to eat them.*

Describe a person who did something innovative:
_____
_____
_____

When did you do something with innovation:
_____
_____
_____

Insight

Insight is learning and understanding the true nature of something by analyzing it. *Paula shared with her daughter some insights she learned about her neighbors after she visited their mosque.*

Write about someone who did something with insight:
_____
_____
_____

When did you have an insight:
_____
_____
_____

Inspiration

Inspiration is a stimulation of the mind or emotions that causes creative activity. *Miguel was inspired to help remodel the youth recreation center when he realized how much the kids always enjoyed seeing him.*

Describe a person who had inspiration:
___
___
___

Write about a time you were inspired to do something:
___
___
___

Integrity

Integrity is a firm adherence to what is right, and not being influenced by what is wrong. *Because Wilfred refused to copy his homework answers, his parents and teachers praised him for his integrity.*

Write about someone who showed integrity:
___
___
___

Write about a time you had integrity:
___
___
___

Intelligence

Intelligence is the ability to learn and apply knowledge. *Julie used her intelligence when she decided to stop associating with her old friends who chose to become smokers.*

Write about someone who did something with intelligence:
___
___
___

When did you act with intelligence:
___
___
___

Intuition

Intuition is instinctively knowing or guessing something by using insight and perception. *Bianca used intuition to figure out that there must have been a miscommunication between the neighbors.*

Describe a time someone showed intuition:
_____
_____
_____

When did you have intuition about something:
_____
_____
_____

Investment

Investment is to put time or effort into something for future benefit or advantage. *Duncan invested a lot of energy into his science project because doing a good job was important to him.*

Describe someone's investment:
_____
_____
_____

When did you invest in something:
_____
_____
_____

Justice

Justice is the impartial and fair upholding of what is moral and right, especially in regards to the law. *Bridgett knew that the judge and jury would serve justice in the form of appropriate and legal punishment to the thieves.*

Describe an example when someone you know was served by justice:
_____
_____
_____

Write about a time you saw justice:
_____
_____
_____

Kindness

Kindness is being nice, warm hearted, considerate, and caring. *Tori's kindness to all animals and even insects influenced her brothers to stop squashing bugs for no reason.*

Describe an example of someone showing kindness:
_____
_____
_____

When did you show kindness to someone:
_____
_____
_____

Leadership

Leadership is the ability to effectively organize and encourage people to achieve a common goal. *Shaughn's leadership skills were recognized when he was able to coordinate the volunteers at the park for the clean up day.*

Describe a person who showed leadership:
_____
_____
_____

What did you do to show leadership:
_____
_____
_____

Love

Love is having strong, tender feelings for someone or something. *Hakim loved his parents, and he loved to spend time with them doing even simple activities.*

Describe a time somebody showed love:
_____
_____
_____

How do you show love:
_____
_____
_____

Loyalty

Loyalty is allegiance and faithful behavior. *Connor was loyal to his best friend; he never teased him even when all the other kids wanted him to.*

Write about someone demonstrating loyalty:

_____
_____
_____

Write about a time you showed loyalty:

_____
_____
_____

Maturity

Maturity is being intelligent and acting one's age. *Haley's parents thought she was mature for her age when she told them that she had decided to watch over and protect the younger children at the bus stop from now on.*

Describe someone who showed maturity:

_____
_____
_____

When did you show maturity:

_____
_____
_____

Moderation

Moderation is knowing when to be satisfied with enough of something. *Kevin used moderation by choosing to not eat all of the candy that was in the package.*

Write about someone who did something with moderation:

_____
_____
_____

When did you practice moderation:

_____
_____
_____

Modesty

Modesty is being humble and not bragging about your achievements. *Instead of telling people how good her paintings were, Carmen was modest and replied with a simple "thank you," when people praised her ability.*

Describe someone who was modest about something they accomplished:
_____
_____
_____

When did you show modesty about an achievement:
_____
_____
_____

Morality

Morality is a person's beliefs about conduct that is right and wrong. *Sabrina realized that her mother and her stepmother had very different ideas about morality.*

Describe a person who demonstrated morality:
_____
_____
_____

What did you do with morality:
_____
_____
_____

Motivation

Motivation is having a desire to accomplish a goal. *Yakov was motivated to write all his thank you notes before his game started.*

Write about a motivated person:
_____
_____
_____

When did you have motivation:
_____
_____
_____

Neatness

Neatness is being clean and free from disorder. *Darren's neatness in his work area inspired his boss to try to keep his own desk clean too.*

Write about a person who practiced neatness:

_____
_____
_____

How did you do something with neatness:

_____
_____
_____

Objectivity

Objectivity is dealing with something without letting personal feelings or prejudices have an influence. *Brandon suspected the night manager was the thief but he conducted the investigation with fairness and objectivity.*

Describe an event where someone was objective:

_____
_____
_____

When did you show objectivity about something:

_____
_____
_____

Openness

Openness is honestly sharing your thoughts and feelings, and being willing to accept suggestions or new ideas. *Kina's openness toward her neighbor's different cultural differences set a positive example for her little sister.*

Describe someone who was showed openness:

_____
_____
_____

When did you demonstrate openness:

_____
_____
_____

Optimism

Optimism is thinking positive thoughts about future events. *Adriana felt optimism about her personal future; she had plans and goals and looked forward to having challenging new experiences.*

Write about someone who had optimism about something:

_____
_____
_____

When were you optimistic about something:

_____
_____
_____

Organization

Organization is being neat and tidy, putting everything in its place. *Charley realized that his life was easier and better with more organization in it.*

Describe how someone's life was organized:

_____
_____
_____

When were you organized:

_____
_____
_____

Ownership

Ownership is personally claiming something. *Moxie was proud to take ownership of the new parent education lessons she created.*

Write about someone who had ownership in something:

_____
_____
_____

When did you feel ownership about something:

_____
_____
_____

Passion

Passion is believing in and having strong, deep feelings for something. *Avi had high expectations and a great passion for teaching his students that they should always try to achieve their maximum potential.*

Write about someone who had passion about something:
_____
_____
_____

What were you passionate about:
_____
_____
_____

Patience

Patience is the ability to accept discomfort or wait for something without complaint. *Matthew waited patiently for the neighbor's dog to stop barking.*

When did you see a person show patience:
_____
_____
_____

When did you have a lot of patience:
_____
_____
_____

Patriotism

Patriotism is love for or devotion to one's country. *Christy felt very patriotic when she saw the flags and the veterans in the parade.*

When did you see someone do something patriotic:
_____
_____
_____

When did you show patriotism:
_____
_____
_____

Performance

Performance is a measure of how something is accomplished. *Alexandro put forth his best effort at the church's fundraiser and everybody noted his very productive performance.*

When did you see someone show performance:
_____
_____
_____

When did you show performance:
_____
_____
_____

Perseverance

Perseverance is a persistent continued effort to achieve a goal despite obstacles. *Isaac showed perseverance and after two years he finally convinced his stepmother that racial diversity should be welcomed, not feared.*

Describe an event where someone had perseverance:
_____
_____
_____

When did you show perseverance:
_____
_____
_____

Personality

Personality is the distinctive qualities, behavior, and character of each individual. *Laura's personality was very different from her husbands' but they got along with other in a great manner.*

Write about a person who showed personality:
_____
_____
_____

When did you show personality:
_____
_____
_____

Persuasiveness

Persuasiveness is the ability to advocate and convince someone of something. *Jason's persuasiveness was effective in convincing his friends to volunteer for the neighborhood clean up that his temple was sponsoring.*

Describe someone who showed persuasiveness:
_____
_____
_____

When were you persuasive:
_____
_____
_____

Planning

Planning is the process of thinking carefully about how to do something. *"Proper planning prevents poor performance..." Sheila's mother always told her.*

Write about a time someone relied on planning:
_____
_____
_____

Describe a time you planned something:
_____
_____
_____

Poise

Poise is behaving in a socially polite and proper way. *Sue showed grace and poise by the way she acted at the dinner party.*

Write about someone who showed poise:
_____
_____
_____

When did you show poise:
_____
_____
_____

Politeness

Politeness is acting in a correct and proper way toward others. *Mark's parents always told him "If you can't be pleasant, at least be polite."*

Write about a time someone showed politeness:

_____

_____

_____

When were you polite:

_____

_____

_____

Potential

Potential is having the capability to accomplish something. *Ephraim saw his sister practice every day and he realized that she was reaching her full potential as a strong competitor.*

Describe someone reaching his or her potential:

_____

_____

_____

Describe an example of you reaching your potential:

_____

_____

_____

Practice

Practice is repeating something to become better at doing it. *Emma knew that if she wanted to become a better musician, she should practice on her piano regularly.*

Describe a time someone practiced something:

_____

_____

_____

What did you practice:

_____

_____

_____

Praise

Praise is verbal reward for an effort. *Doug praised his eldest son for overcoming the adversity of the new and unpleasant boss with patience and tolerance.*

Describe a time somebody showed praise:

_____
_____
_____

How did you praise somebody:

_____
_____
_____

Preparedness

Preparedness is planning ahead to be ready for something that may or may not happen. *Jack didn't know if there was going to be an earthquake soon, but he was prepared for a power outage.*

Describe an example of somebody being prepared:

_____
_____
_____

Write about a time you prepared for an event:

_____
_____
_____

Preservation

Preservation is to keep or protect something in its original or current state. *Tina was so shocked at all the pollution that she joined a volunteer preservation group to help save the environment.*

Describe someone you know who worked to preserve something:

_____
_____
_____

What have you preserved:

_____
_____
_____

Prevention

Prevention is the act of taking advance measure to stop or interrupt something from happening. *Marcia's bicycle helmet was good prevention against a head injury if she were to have any kind of an accident on her bicycle.*

Write about a person who prevented something:
_____
_____
_____

When did you practice prevention:
_____
_____
_____

Pride

Pride is having pleasure or satisfaction in a person or an accomplishment. *Bill took pride in his work; he always finished his chores, and he always did the best job that he was capable of performing.*

When did somebody feel pride about something they did:
_____
_____
_____

When did you feel pride:
_____
_____
_____

Priorities

Priorities are tasks or goals that need to be done before other things are started or finished. *Glen's priorities were peacefully settling the disagreements between his friends; after that he would work on his project.*

Describe someone's priorities:
_____
_____
_____

When did you have priorities:
_____
_____
_____

Privacy

Privacy is the state of being alone and free from intrusion from other people. *Yoshi understood his mother's need for privacy when she asked to be left alone for a little while.*

When did someone give you privacy:

_____
_____
_____

When did you respect someone else's privacy:

_____
_____
_____

Proactive

Proactive is acting in anticipation of a future event in an effort to control a situation. *Patricia heard that the boys wanted to fight each other, so she chose to be proactive by calling them in to her office right away.*

Write about someone who did something proactive:

_____
_____
_____

What did you do that was proactive:

_____
_____
_____

Professionalism

Professionalism is courteous, businesslike behavior. *Mahmoud often acted silly with his family but he was very professional when he went to work and talked with his customers.*

Describe someone who did something with professionalism:

_____
_____
_____

What did you do with professionalism:

_____
_____
_____

Proficiency

Proficiency is having great knowledge, skill, or experience in doing something. *Roho was an excellent store security guard; he was very proficient at catching shoplifters.*

Write about someone who showed proficiency:
_____
_____
_____

When did you do something with proficiency:
_____
_____
_____

Punctuality

Punctuality is the quality or state of being prompt and on time. *Angelo was not always punctual with his appointments, which caused him to lose clients.*

When did someone demonstrate punctuality:
_____
_____
_____

When did you show punctuality:
_____
_____
_____

Readiness

Readiness is the state of being prepared for a situation. *Teree's extensive emergency planning procedures showed that her group was in a high state of readiness.*

Write about a time someone demonstrated readiness:
_____
_____
_____

When did you show readiness:
_____
_____
_____

Reasonableness

Reasonableness is being rational, showing good judgment and common sense, and not being extreme or excessive. *Kishori was reasonable when he confronted the bully; he did not hit him or yell at him.*

Write about somebody you know who showed reasonableness:

_____
_____
_____

When were you reasonable about something:

_____
_____
_____

Recognition

Recognition is awareness and acknowledgement given to a person for something they've done. *Grace was recognized by her teacher for her active cooperation in solving the disagreement in a non-violent manner.*

Describe someone who demonstrated recognition:

_____
_____
_____

What did you do to show recognition to somebody:

_____
_____
_____

Reconciliation

Reconciliation is the ability and process to restore a friendship or relationship after a disagreement. *When Nancy forgave her neighbor and reconciled their friendship, they both felt much better.*

Write about a time when someone demonstrated reconciliation:

_____
_____
_____

When did you demonstrate reconciliation:

_____
_____
_____

Reliability

Reliability is the quality of being predictable, dependable, and trusted. *Because Celene always did what she said she would do, her friends knew that she valued reliability.*

Describe a time when someone demonstrated reliability:
_____
_____
_____

When did you show reliability:
_____
_____
_____

Reputation

Reputation is a person's projected or suspected image (good or bad) that other people may think of them. *Alaina knew that if she chose to associate with that group of girls, her reputation could be affected.*

Describe how someone got a reputation:
_____
_____
_____

Write about a time when your reputation changed:
_____
_____
_____

Resilience

Resilience is the ability to recover quickly from or adjust to a setback. *Amanda felt bad about arriving late for the activities but her resilient nature helped her to catch up without feeling overwhelmed.*

Write about a person who demonstrated resilience:
_____
_____
_____

When did you do something that showed resilience:
_____
_____
_____

Resourcefulness

Resourcefulness is the ability to act effectively and creatively to accomplish a goal. *Everybody was glad that Lorena was a parent volunteer at the school; she was very resourceful at obtaining valuable fund raising prizes.*

Write about someone who did something resourceful:

_____
_____
_____

When were you resourceful:

_____
_____
_____

Respect

Respect is giving high or special regard to someone. *Sharie deeply respected her grandmother because she was wise, mature, and shared her knowledge and love with her.*

Write about an example of someone showing respect:

_____
_____
_____

Describe a time you showed respect to someone:

_____
_____
_____

Responsibility

Responsibility is being obligated to do something that is expected. *Mary was reminded that she was responsible for controlling her own behavior.*

Write about a time someone showed responsibility:

_____
_____
_____

Write about a time you showed responsibility:

_____
_____
_____

Restraint

Restraint is to control, hold back, and limit or restrict an action or response. *Yvonne restrained herself from using bad words when she got very angry at her brother.*

Write about a time you saw someone show restraint:

_____
_____
_____

What did you do with restraint:

_____
_____
_____

Sacrifice

Sacrifice is giving something up to achieve or acquire something else. *Kellen knew that in order to save money for a new keyboard, he'd have to make a sacrifice and not spend any more money on video games.*

When did you see someone make a sacrifice:

_____
_____
_____

What did you do that required a sacrifice:

_____
_____
_____

Satisfaction

Satisfaction is being happy and content with what you have. *Laurence smiled with satisfaction when he fixed his old bicycle; now he didn't need or want a newer model.*

Describe a time when someone was satisfied:

_____
_____
_____

Describe a time when you had satisfaction:

_____
_____
_____

Security

Security is feeling safe and confident. *Ron liked his new job and he especially liked the financial security of having a guaranteed paycheck every two weeks.*

Describe somebody who had security:
_____
_____
_____

When did you have security:
_____
_____
_____

Self Esteem

Self esteem is how you feel about yourself. *Rose explained to her friends that people with high self esteem feel good about themselves and they don't do things to put themselves in danger, like using illegal drugs.*

When did you see someone's self esteem change:
_____
_____
_____

Describe an event that affected your self esteem:
_____
_____
_____

Sensitivity

Sensitivity is being aware of, and acting appropriately to other people's feelings. *When Chong's pet died, his friends showed sensitivity to his sad feelings.*

When did someone show sensitivity:
_____
_____
_____

How have you shown sensitivity:
_____
_____
_____

Sharing

To share is to divide and distribute something. *Mr. Kelly listened to coach David's request for a place to play soccer and he decided that he would gladly share his open field with the team.*

What did somebody share something with you:
___
___
___

When did you share something:
___
___
___

Sincerity

Sincerity is the quality or condition of being honest and genuine. *Trevor's stepmother accepted his sincere apology for earning such a low grade on his school project.*

Write about a time you saw someone show sincerity:
___
___
___

When did you do something with sincerity:
___
___
___

Skepticism

Skepticism is deciding to not entirely believe something heard or seen without more information. *When Kalidas heard the rumor she was skeptical that she was hearing a factual and accurate story.*

Describe an example of someone being skeptical:
___
___
___

When did you have skepticism:
___
___
___

Spirituality

Spirituality is the beliefs and feelings about one's religion. *The art show judges commented that Jorge's paintings clearly reflected his deep sense of spirituality and devotion to God.*

Describe someone who showed spirituality:
_____
_____
_____

What did you do that showed your spirituality:
_____
_____
_____

Sportsmanship

Sportsmanship is fair, respectful, and gracious conduct while participating in a sport. *Marlena exhibited great sportsmanship when her team lost; she showed grace and maturity by congratulating the winners.*

When did you see someone demonstrate sportsmanship:
_____
_____
_____

When did you show good sportsmanship:
_____
_____
_____

Stability

Stability is having control and calmness in your life. *Troy used to have a lot of different jobs and homes, but when he settled down in one place he greatly enjoyed the stability and freedom from stress.*

Write about someone who had stability in some part of his or her life:
_____
_____
_____

Write about a time when you had stability in your life:
_____
_____
_____

Strength

Strength is the quality or state of being strong and having power in body and mind. *"Dan showed remarkable strength," said the professor, "when he refused to give up."*

Write about someone you know who acted with mental strength:

_____
_____
_____

When did you show mental strength:

_____
_____
_____

Sympathy

Sympathy is understanding and feeling compassion for another person. *Sophia knew what it was like to have a death in the family, so she was able to sympathize with her friend's loss.*

Describe a time someone showed sympathy:

_____
_____
_____

When did you show sympathy:

_____
_____
_____

Tact

Tact is knowing the right thing to do or say at the right time. *Lars was tactful and waited until he was alone with his boss to tell him that none of the employees liked the new program.*

When did you see someone use tact:

_____
_____
_____

When were you tactful:

_____
_____
_____

Talent

Talent is a natural ability to do a special thing well. *Sarah's mother said that although everyone has skills, some people have to work a bit harder to discover what their own talent is.*

Write about someone who had a special talent:

_____
_____
_____

What talent do you have:

_____
_____
_____

Teamwork

Teamwork is working together with others to achieve a common goal. *Kobach knew he would need teamwork to get all of the boxes loaded into the truck on time.*

Write about something that was accomplished with teamwork:

_____
_____
_____

When did you use teamwork:

_____
_____
_____

Tenacity

Tenacity is being tough and persistent about something. *Raji's father smiled and he told his son "Be tenacious and don't ever give up!"*

Write about someone who showed tenacity:

_____
_____
_____

Describe a time when you had tenacity:

_____
_____
_____

Timing

Timing is doing something at the best moment for the best effect. *Garrett used good timing; he brought his mother some flowers when he found out she was having a bad day.*

Write about a time someone demonstrated good timing:

_____
_____
_____

When did you have good timing:

_____
_____
_____

Tolerance

Tolerance is willingness to recognize and respect different things. *Because Jean had lived overseas, she learned to have a lot of respect and tolerance toward people from different ethnic cultures and backgrounds.*

Write about a time someone demonstrated tolerance:

_____
_____
_____

Write about a time you showed tolerance:

_____
_____
_____

Trust

Trust is having confidence, assurance, and faith in a person, or a person's actions. *Eugenito could trust his son to always wear eye protection when he needed to.*

Write about a time someone showed trust:

_____
_____
_____

Write about a time you showed trust:

_____
_____
_____

Trustworthiness

Trustworthiness is being dependable and worthy of confidence. *Because Keith was always on time and always told the truth, his partner felt that he was trustworthy.*

Describe a person who demonstrated trustworthiness:
___
___
___

When did you demonstrate trustworthiness:
___
___
___

Truth

Truth is conformity to a true fact, or sincerity in the things you do and say. *Because Martin always told the truth, his family and friends trusted and admired him.*

Write about a time someone told the truth:
___
___
___

Write about a time you told the truth:
___
___
___

Variety

Variety is an assortment or number of different things. *Karen tried hard to expose her children to a variety of different activities to keep their minds stimulated.*

Describe someone who incorporates variety into his or her life:
___
___
___

Describe an example of variety in your life:
___
___
___

Veracity

Veracity is sincere devotion to the truth. *Everybody admired Ken's veracity; they all remembered that he never made a promise he didn't keep and that he always fulfilled his promises.*

Write about someone who showed veracity:

_____
_____
_____

When did you have veracity:

_____
_____
_____

Vision

Vision is the ability to plan ahead and imagine something positive. *Camile walked into the new classroom and had vision; she would work hard and complete the course with high grades.*

Write about someone who showed vision about something:

_____
_____
_____

Describe a time you had a vision of something you could do:

_____
_____
_____

Visualization

Visualization is imagining positive mental images in your mind. *Shaneeka's athletic workouts always included a quiet period of mental practice in which she used visualization techniques to help improve her performance.*

Write about an instance when someone practiced visualization:

_____
_____
_____

When did visualizing something help you:

_____
_____
_____

Vitality

Vitality is an enduring, healthy capacity for vigorous activity. *Casey demonstrated great vitality when she quickly recovered from the illness and then began to train regularly for the marathon.*

Describe somebody who demonstrated vitality:

_____
_____
_____

When did you do something with vitality:

_____
_____
_____

Willingness

Willingness is accepting something voluntarily and without reluctance. *Carl showed an eager willingness to work with his grandfather in his engine shop.*

Write about a time somebody showed willingness:

_____
_____
_____

When did you demonstrate willingness:

_____
_____
_____

Willpower

Willpower is using the strength of your mind to control yourself and accomplish something. *Alex needed willpower to keep his mind focused on finishing the race.*

Write about a time someone used willpower to accomplish something:

_____
_____
_____

Write about a time you had willpower:

_____
_____
_____

Wisdom

Wisdom is having knowledge, common sense, and good judgment. *Ben learned that older people generally have more maturity and wisdom than younger people.*

Describe an instance where someone showed wisdom:

_____
_____
_____

When did you show wisdom:

_____
_____
_____

Youthfulness

Youthfulness is having the enthusiasm, vigor, and vitality of a young person. *Gaylen's great-grandmother showed an amazing youthfulness of character at the last family picnic.*

Describe a person who acted with youthfulness:

_____
_____
_____

What is something you do that shows youthfulness:

_____
_____
_____

Zeal

Zeal is eagerness in the pursuit of a goal. *When Ted finished his latest project ahead of schedule, his parents said it was because he worked with such a high amount of energy and zeal.*

Write about a time somebody showed zeal:

_____
_____
_____

Write about a time when you had zeal:

_____
_____
_____